I0756333

FINISHING LINE PRESS
www.finishinglinepress.com

Passing Tones

poems by

Ben Gunsberg

Music and Soundscapes by Max Otto Matzen

Finishing Line Press
Georgetown, Kentucky

Passing Tones

ISBN 979-8-89990-487-5 First Edition

ACKNOWLEDGMENTS

Grateful acknowledgment is made to the editors of the following periodicals, in which these poems first appeared, some with different titles:

Apricity Magazine, "Dream Solo"
Atlanta Review, "Elegy for Lead Guitar"
Glint Literary Journal, "John Hardy" and "Non-Self"
Gulf Stream Magazine, "Pillow"
Ilanot Review, "Dusk"
Prompt Press, "Spoon"
Red Wheelbarrow, "Marshland Orpheus"
Spoon River Poetry Review, "Good Mix"

Publisher: Leah Huete de Maines

Editor: Christen Kincaid

Cover Art: Stanton Macdonald-Wright, American (1927-2007), #20 The Sound of a Cracked Temple Bell is Also Hot Under a Summer Moon, 1966-1967. (detail) [if applicable]. Woodblock print on mulberry paper. 18 x 21.5 inches. Gift of the Stanton and Jean Macdonald-Wright Estate. Collection of the Nora Eccles Harrison Museum of Art, Utah State University

Author Photo: Niki Baldwin

Cover Design: Elizabeth Maines McCleavy

Order online: www.finishinglinepress.com
also available on amazon.com

Author inquiries and mail orders:
Finishing Line Press
PO Box 1626
Georgetown, Kentucky 40324
USA

Contents

Elegy for Lead Guitar 1

Etude for Woodshedding 2

Cell Song 4

Weathering 6

Marshland Orpheus 7

Non-Self 8

Drum Undrum 9

John Hardy 10

Realist Day Jobs 11

Benediction 12

Record Keeping 13

Brazilian Rosewood 14

Bus Rhythm Entrainment 15

Elegy for Lead Vocals 16

Rope for a Snake 18

Pillow 19

Dream Solo 20

Good Mix 21

Passing Tone 22

Dusk 23

Daughter Io 24

Another Still Life 25

Waterwheel Song 26

Spoon Song 27

for Andrea, Maya, and Isaac

Elegy for Lead Guitar

To friends who ask how long, you say
a few years or a few hours, enough time
for memory to slip past sluggish tumors
clogging your cortex and tour this rich
and wicked country with Marshall amps
and a black ES-335. New Orleans,
Clarksdale, Kansas City—blues began
before you learned to bend notes down
in that basement where you dozed
on a fold-out couch, chipped tiles bristling
your throat with asbestos. You woke to
vinyl teasing midnight shuffles overhead,
warbled needle tempting you to stand,
climb stairs, enter a kitchen born of light
and sudden heat. Muddy Waters played
and you greased your tongue with bacon,
faked a growl, wrote lines about transitory
Beauty who comes on strong: *More sugar,*
in that coffee, baby? "Mannish Boy" stuck—
an endless loop. "Mannish Boy" strummed
hard enough to snap strings and shock
a tuning fork. You stole a lick from King,
ripped bluegrass drunk on Kentucky's
coarsest spirits, stashed bottles behind
a neighbor's honeysuckle. In one frame,
you're slumped over the Gibson. Green
cargo pants. Aviator shades. Everything
oversized. Gain and volume maxed at ten.
Music hurt when I was young, but now
I share your greed for sensory oblivion
at breakneck speed. Screaming feedback
echoes through the gray and balding men
who gather round your bed—
one who lost a leg, one who lost a son,
one who can't afford hearing aids shouts
old verses on your shrinking body.

Etude for Woodshedding

1.

The boy stacks fuel behind the shed,
head high, staggered at the corners.
Each log twice-split,
clean, blonde grain,
edges chipped.
By the time he's done,
he's taller than himself.
The shed looms red
as a new wound.
Why he pulls one
from the bottom row—
I don't know—
maybe he lives
to test a theory
of ruin. And the top
leans into collapse.
He sees it tumble,
not angry,
just measuring
what remains:
dust on his jeans,
dents in the grass.

2.

He plays the same phrase again—twice
as loud this time—hammering
the G like it owes him lost
time. The shed
answers with dust
and fluorescent hum.
Then he blows,
lets the bell
squall—almost
forgetting the weight

of his own breath.
He listens, rewinds,
listens again.
Hears it falter—
swing too square,
grace note clipped.
He deletes the take,
not out of anger,
just a kind of math
practice makes:
build, subtract,
divide by one
who's listening.

Cell Song

O divides and divides a-
gain and gains what lives
lives of halves half of hal-
ves again a gain of one

more second selves akin
new skin seams over
old drum pulse that all
calls back to whole one

boneward row wraps
pip pink marrow cell an-
other O splits one then
two then two more on-

ward cells make what
makes one whole then
old again slopes limbs
one living coil threads

ends tight whorl ties
O and O in one divide
divides the whole again
your circle never still is-

sues new tissue bloom
doom dark tomb roots
out in situe curls through
quiet brain what ache

stocks strange stray O
corks duct chains vein
O core organ now un-
bound blind and wild

moan stuns thick still
ill go O go divide wh-
at once was whole what
once was

Weathering

Haggard's voice on a jukebox in Cheyenne
singing about mama's hungry eyes
that stared down wheatfield winters
while the family tractor rusted in the yard.

Frank Lloyd Wright refused to build basements
after the Great Chicago Fire, convinced
the ground itself held all the ruin one needed.

Down in Galveston, a seawall stands defiant,
but you can still smell the hurricane
buried in the salt air, a history of breaking
and bending to fit the shape of wind.

In Kyoto, temple carpenters, who know earth
will convulse again, still carve wooden beams
by hand, their tools ringing like old bells.

Marshland Orpheus

I miss the brassy chime of your guitar—glitter
washed off the treble, bass emptied of dark rum.
Dry heat split the spruce a luthier said. Happens

this time of year. *He's snapped* or *he's cracked,*
we think. How many hours strummed?
If only someone loosened strings—

what difference does it make? Lacking tension,
nothing rings. Waves cease. Cords go slack. Gulls
roost their saltmarsh nests. Black-bellied plovers

warble near the rocks. You practiced every day
in this small, rented box, praying money might relax
and half-diminished scales might rest. Before the top

recessed, before this breach, I heard you swing
between high and low E, bob downstream then rise
like a heron. You played until your wrist ached,

until the scalloped braces jerked. Shudders spread
across the soundboard, echoed off your rosewood
back. Music never quit those callused hands,

the force behind each chord you gripped—
your will to bend, its will to break. What more
could hold the final note refusing its sustain?

Non-Self

I don't remember when this "I" arrived
out of the "you," my young mind still
a puzzle, but I guess it all makes sense
in the ancient way sweetness fits the mouth.

Out of the "you," I hear, *the mind's a puzzle*
still. Whose dry lips extend this kiss?
What ancient sweetness fills my mouth
as I invent the sound I hope to hear? Whistling,

my pursed lips extend a kiss toward crows
and cattails roughing up a little breeze.
The self I hope to hear invents this whistling
me who rings another loop around the lake,

where crows rough up a little breeze
and willows swish their skirts. Who else
rings inside this man who loops the lake?
He's more than halfway home. Remember

willows swish their skirts. Remember,
too, the sweet-sweet whistler whom I was
once, who's more than halfway home,
who loops the lake as if he could repeat

the *sweet-sweet* sounds of who he was.
An ancient tone precedes the whistling self
who loops the lake, who's trying to return
but can't remember when or how or why.

Drum Undrum

a drum does not
pray like a flute
does not open
its mouth to beg
does not lie down
does not wait for wind
a drum is struck
or it is not
a drum is not
a hollowed reed
not a throat filled
with breath or mercy
but stretched hide
callus time tensed
over void and one
plays by lifting then
lowering hands
giving oneself
to skin held or free-
standing silence
waits for thunder
to find it

John Hardy

There's a bridge on the West Virginia line
where old-time fiddlers claim a dangerous man
tried to slip away. Instead, he wound up hanging
from a tune I've known since I played spoons
against my papa's knee. Someone sang
and I banged along, fired by two guns
John Hardy carried every day and the image
of a child skipping through an old jail yard,
trace of John H. glued to me unable to escape
the harm I've done, deputy trying to reel me in,
mother trying to pay my bail, a blue-dress girl
sings, "I still love you, poor boy."
Appalachian fog exhausts her name,
while John Hardy rides four chords through 4/4
time—da-da-da-da—just listen to that chestnut
mare drum loamy earth toward an imaginary
line between two states. If they catch him
on the great stone bridge (they catch him
every time), he'll hang barefoot from a wide oak
bough, his tongue unbelled, yet the outlaw ballad
still carries like an ember, one barn dance
to another. *Take me to my hanging ground,*
Lord, Lord, says John, in his last, throat-tight verse
because he knows no one remembers a body
that goes scot-free. Why else unsaddle his mare,
empty all six chambers, linger in the wide oak's
dire shade until hounds bay and fiddlers bow
and a singer's voice carries across the river.

Realist Day Jobs

When frost appears plausible as frost
along power lines, you eat hard bread
and mottled salami, scrape vomit
off my crib. Grout tile, caulk sink,
lean back against a brick wall,
blue haze rising off your cigarette.

When boots descend like Brouwer's
peasants, paint resembles actual
basements, Thursdays, fathers living
or dead. You stand eight hours, stuffing
circuits into plastic, warned not to touch
your eyes without showering first.

You plunge wood in lacquer and bleed
your hands with bristling solvent, earn
$8.50 shoveling sawdust into burlap,
reach for thin envelopes of credit
that follow apartment to apartment.
The Fender Champ goes for fifty bucks,

the Gibson for a song. Still, you stir
sloshing contents of a pot, spoon milk-
soaked oats into my mouth, wipe my chin
with your sleeve, step over trash
damming the door—down the staircase,
new syringe, old jacket pocket.

Benediction

For comfort, for pleasure, why not drive
west to Honeyville Hot Springs, tithe ten
bucks, and share a soak with strangers
skipping work—or maybe it's a holiday
you've forgotten. Faint echo of parade,
ribboned oaks, some pagan festival
you failed to mark. Pray scalding pots
might soothe your crooked neck, thaw
the body's frigid providence as you chat
with lovers who blot brows and drain
cool from glass bottles. Sulfur whiff,
dissolved salt. No tumor stalks. No
whisper of glioma. These bore holes,
tapped for comfort and pleasure, soften
error as they unscroll kinked vertebrae,
each minute a reminder mercy warms
communal water. Easy now. Easy now
to enter. Twitching calves, thighs so deep
one fades into stinging comfort, pleasure—
if that's a word for pluming steam
and mineral vigor streamed into light's
shared pool. Sloshing, sloshing, it spills
and spills you over.

Record Keeping

Only olive trees heard Jesus weep
at Gethsemane. They could do nothing,
so they kept growing and growing,
their roots winding through soil
while swords clanged in the distance.

The first man who built a piano died
in obscurity, his creation too fragile
for concert halls. Centuries later,
a Steinway crossed the Atlantic
on a ship that split in two,
the waves swallowing it whole.

1930, Kurt Gerron sang "Mack the Knife,"
his baritone spending gold freely. Later,
the Nazis marched him to Theresienstadt,
where they made him direct propaganda
films before gassing him in Auschwitz.

On a porch in Mississippi, a girl strings
chicken wire between posts, plucks
a melody she'll never record. For this,
cicadas everywhere hum louder at dusk.

Brazilian Rosewood

> *Plants, parts, products, or derivatives may be used in commercial trade only if presented with documentation.*
>
> —*CITES Timber Species Manual*

These time-tuned rings marble red to dry-
blood black, wood so dense, when tapped,
it pings like brass. Or maybe *ping's* too poor
a sound. Call it *lush.* Call it *opulent.* Most
old-growth stands reduced to ash—a bed
for plotted oil palm. The lavish loss of soil
and clean air means few trees bloom—
their balance dips each year. A master luthier
once planed rough boards to scallop-brace
my antique instrument. A crime to harvest
now, I hear, strumming what was built before
the law, knowing why demand's so high—
these overtones a luxury, a summoning
to save the vanished world and call it mine.

Bus-Rhythm Entrainment

One born to keep time
taps pencils against a
vinyl seat, each beat
drawn into the same
orbit. This is the life I
want—to belong so
fully to a rumble I can't
control, pulse too big
for one body. Driver
coughs. Mother sways
with child who hiccups
two seats ahead. The
bottle slips its spell or
logic, rolls nervously
toward the front, and
I thread my vision
into the aisle's black
channel, silence
and stillness synced
to a shared pause
between *someone*
should do something
and everyone rising.

Elegy for Lead Vocals

When you can't walk around the block or rock
around the clock or shake your moneymaker
anymore, let your senseless body lapse in bed,
and roll your spirit back to Asbury Park, circa
1976, when streetlamps glossed your Firebird
and fuzzy dice swayed from rearview mirrors,
Bon Scott's blitzkrieg vocals shearing tweeters
as you drop the clutch. Peel out and race
a snarling flock of Hell's Angels—dark wings
inked with skulls and Celtic crosses—home.

Leather vest, drum-tight tee, Robert Plant
screams "FREE!" to mute last rites and mum
a hospice nurse, who muffles your throttled
ears with Percocet. You're high as hell,
so how in God's name does Roy Orbison's
"Mean Old World" still spin? Why do girls
in tight skirts and cowboy boots harmonize
"Born to Die?" Those blues make you hang
your head and cry. Forget Roy's skinny tie
funeral suit. Unbridle Jaco's thuggish bass
to thump-thump time's self-pitying silence.

How long, friend, since you sold the Firebird?
Nowhere else to roll. No soulful eggs to devil.
Hendrix and his white Strat left the tunnel
years ago. "Purple Haze," Jimmy Page, "Whole
Lotta Love" all seem out of phase. Maybe
Roy was right about the world's dark stage,
no spotlight nimbus for your tumored brain.
Confused, you mumble lyrics for "Suzanne"
as "The End" replays: warm beer, dazed
youth adrift Manzarek's eerie organ riff.

You sway, night after night, solo mic stand
solemn as a 1, pluck G and D on your cherry-
red Les Paul, but it's unplugged, so all you hear
is click, click—plastic pick on flat-wound string.
Listen, man, I have a plan to backwards spin
this sad-sack soundtrack. First, we'll hotwire
the old Firebird and torque its cast-iron-block
V8 down Woodward Ave. to Motown where
we'll kick off life's revival tour. I'll be your manager.

We'll sell out every U.S. hotspot—Red Rocks,
Tower Theater, Hollywood Bowl. You'll shake
rattle and roll until dull stars gleam again
like Vegas Elvis, astral rhinestones blinking choral
light above a roofless playhouse. Marshall Stacks
ahum. James Brown's "Good God!" in time
with Hank's holy yodel, Roy's mean old world
outshined by Queen's face-peeling rapture.
Nothing left to do but shed your skin and blast
a mighty yawp into orbit while ears below ride
the fleeting rocket of your vast vibrato.

Rope for a Snake

The moon's edge frays over the ridge,
a silver filament against dusk.
You stood once, jaw-hinge tense,
its skein coiled in your rough hands.

What you know now is not what held you
then, the dry rasp of scales replaced
by a slip of hemp, the way loss unwinds
loss, grows soft even in the dark.

Pillow

You deserve more than just enough morphine
to halter the red-eyed mare. More than this

clean, plush thing your head imprints post-split
and exorcism of lymph nodes. More than swift

renewal of soft tissue and the infinite view
from a hospital room on the fourteenth floor.

More than parched hours spent sponging your lips,
you deserve a bite of sausage, good coffee, chocolate

éclair, the stubborn memory of Yiddish, a chorus
of chickens, pink orchids climbing the sun's trellis—

anything to distract while thinning your cells
for months. An old boardwalk softened by mist

returns with its grey tenements, for something must
explain patience to young streetlamps trying to rinse

the asphalt of darkness. You deserve Westbrook Mall,
where bargain hunters stockpile wool socks, porcelain

dolls, and vanishing cream. Though you can't eat
solid food, you deserve a discount on blueberries.

Though you won't speak or open your eyes,
you deserve a brisk travel agent to book

a private tour, the trip to Egypt you thought canceled:
transatlantic flight, then a slow walk through scentless

desert with your partner, to whom you cling,
who clings to you like a tuft of dogged clover.

Dream Solo

Remember the Pleistocene Lake before it shrank
and stilled into this desert basin. Remember the fern-
fresh world all wet with sound. Before ribbon mic
and magnetic tape, a herd of pachyderms stomped
the continent, dropped heavy tracks—whole
albums—in permafrost. Then they disappeared.

What if one remained? Paleolithic time-traveler,
copper hair draped over mammoth shanks.
He hasn't loved a mate in ten thousand years.
He feeds on roots and leaves, closes his eyes,
blows "Extinction Blues." The same wind
that grooves sandstone just to feel movement

etches the pewter surface of a pond, soothes
a lone bull elk who drags his antlers through
sagebrush, balms Galileo's nerves as he bends
over his telescope and traces heaven's curve,
knowing no one will believe him. So much living
happens through stubborn force and simple pleasure.

Jung's last recorded words, "Let's have a really good
red wine tonight," sink into the silent herd, forgets
itself, then returns a hirsute dream—pachyderm
who won't mute when others stow their instruments
and slump under great Bristlecones of sleep. This one,
most gentle one, raises trunk to smoky air, sings.

Good Mix

Put good microphones in front of good people
and get out of the way. The hush sounds good.
Drums and bass sound good. Even the silent
seconds needed to tune a guitar sound good.

Get out of the way. The hush sounds good.
Record what flies out of your mouth. Replay
silence needed to tune a guitar. Sounds good
through speakers, through headphones. Good

record of what flies out of your mouth. Replay
laughter. Replay "Love, love!" Replay "Welcome"
through speakers, through headphones. Good
arrives like buds amidst crackling frost. Replay

laughter. Replay "Amour!" Replay "Bem-Vindo."
We're making a record, tending the good mix,
nurturing buds amidst crackling frost. Rewind
the old comfort, the old guard. Elders, children,

we're making a record, tending the good mix
for those at risk, giving anyone who trembles
old comforts. Children guard the elders, good
dogs guard good rooms, where we record

for those at risk, giving anyone who trembles
drum and bass—good sounds. Even strangers
faraway feel the pulse of our good mix,
through waves, through flesh—*asha, espoir, speranza!*

Passing Tone

First snow dissolves before it lands,
each flake a translucent note
wind forgets mid-phrase.

Grass lies damp, unconvinced,
bent like buckled script
beneath the feet of a child

chasing a kite. Why fly anything
in such wicked weather?
The song offers no answer.

I don't know why it pulls
against the line—how tension
resolves, what the child passes

through—only that struggle
must amuse you, Maestro,
until this gust gives out.

Dusk

I'm sitting on the porch, glass of wine in hand,
watching my child balance on a chicken crate
in the middle of the road. Her eyes are closed.

She sings along with Billie Holiday singing about drinking
in alleys. She's singing about not wanting to go home.
She's singing about having nowhere to go but forward.

I'm looking at my daughter, who is ten years old,
already as wise as me, and I'm looking at the street
beyond her, at the path where she'll walk home

from school, and I'm thinking about how much blood
has been spilled on this street since we've lived here,
how many spills have gone unseen, how much love

enters from beyond the margins, seeps under
walls into our yard, how much blood drips off
our roof and into our garden. I see it as clearly

as I see those who walk past our home, some drowning,
others safe from the river but not from themselves,
some smiling at my daughter, who transforms the crate

into a stage and, God bless this child, gathers courage.

Daughter Io

My universe wants space and silence
more than music, so I muffle noise, extend
the tripod's legs, angle skyward, adjust
my lens to coil light's multilayered braid
around the old moon's empty sandbox,
edges imprecise as fingerpaint. Syntax
dense, too, this child-matter spun complex.
From here, the quiet eye looks brighter
than before. I oscillate the telescope
back to when life pulsed down the hall,
one year from this chair—so near, I saw
her shine with naked eyes, close enough
to map her surface ripples—smile, scowl.
What did she feel for our spiraling world?

Another Still Life

I find you backlit by a streetlamp,
shadow-laddered against the wall,
your coat a ripple of old canvas
and stray threads, flaring out
like it might just fly to Nashville.
I want you to move or melt or flicker
in the alley's half-lit grin. I'm willing
your fingers to stir, your hand to rise,
tap against the glass. I'm willing
your long shadow to peel free
from the pavement, lift like film
caught in an evening draft, a leaf
to skitter past, cling to your collar,
brittle edge catching on the fabric.
I'm waiting for you to brush it off
and acknowledge I'm waiting, trying
to unhook myself from your silhouette,
your folded paper, your backdrop
of crumbled mortar—everything
that holds me here, anchored,
waiting to slip free of the weight
I've placed in this quiet image,
because I can't bear for you to vanish
because you've already vanished.

Waterwheel Song

mind doesn't know what
what sets
what sets in
what sets in motion
only that it must
turn over and over
into this moment
how the wheel
spins the belt
the belt the gear
the gear the great
millstone each
paddle pulling
the next into being
until air trembles
with purpose
as
as if
as if it might
as if it might guide
an ear into granite's
rough grunt
the hand
the eye
eyelash
eyelash-thin
wisps of chaff

Spoon Song

Non fui, fui, non sum, non curo
—Epicurean epitaph

The knife never sweetened a mug
nor cradled a steaming egg, never
scooped mousse nor cantaloupe ripe
with hallelujahs. The soft world
welcomes you like lips
welcome cream. No fight ends
with your bite because you bare
no teeth. No need for a sheath.
No war began by invoking your name
which rhymes with moon. No fear
as I pass you to my young niece.
You slip my tongue, so I clack you
against my knee, sing "Old Joe Clark,"
fiddle-dee-dum,
fiddle-dee-dee-dee.
Dishrag loves you. Soap loves you
three at a time. You stir fresh
mint into water, ice, and sugar,
soothe my daughter when she falls
in the gutter. You draw broth
from a boiling vat and snap
because plastic cools too soon,
drop cornmeal onto greased griddles
then relax coated in mush. All afternoon
coated in mush. Washed and propped
upright on the drying rack, you throw
light across the kitchen. At night
you toss salad until slick with oil
and vinegar, flecked with parsley.
Innocent with bisque.
Innocent with cocoa and salt,
brown into white. Dust into dust,
your bowl delights because pleasure

is good, pain evil. Isn't that right,
my bright, little hedonist?
Though you tarnish, though you bend,
once deprived of sentience,
the end means nothing.

Ben Gunsberg is an Associate Professor of English at Utah State University. He earned an MFA from the University of Alabama and a PhD from the University of Michigan, where he was the Sylvia Duffy Engle Graduate Student Fellow at the Institute for the Humanities.

He is the author of *Welcome, Dangerous Life* (Turning Point Press) and the chapbook *Rhapsodies with Portraits* (Finishing Line Press). His poems have appeared in *Poetry Daily, DIAGRAM, Mid-American Review*, and many other literary magazines.

His work has been honored by the Utah Division of Arts and Museums and the Great River Shakespeare Festival. His manuscript *Cut Time* won the University of Michigan's Hopwood Award for Poetry Writing. He lives in Logan, Utah, at the foot of the Bear River Mountains.

www.ingramcontent.com/pod-product-compliance
Lightning Source LLC
LaVergne TN
LVHW090541110826
845146LV00003B/1208

* 9 7 9 8 8 9 9 9 0 4 8 7 5 *